THE TRADITION

ALSO BY JERICHO BROWN

The New Testament

Please

JERICHO BROWN

THE TRADITION

COPPER CANYON PRESS

PORT TOWNSEND, WASHINGTON

Cover art: L. Ralphi Burgess, *You're in the Middle of the World*, ca. 2017,
acrylic and mixed media, 18" × 25"

Copper Canyon Press is in residence at Fort Worden State Park in Port
Townsend, Washington, under the auspices of Centrum. Centrum is a
gathering place for artists and creative thinkers from around the world,
students of all ages and backgrounds, and audiences seeking extraordinary
cultural enrichment.

LIBRARY OF CONGRESS CATALOGING-IN-PUBLICATION DATA
Names: Brown, Jericho, author.
Title: The tradition / Jericho Brown.
Description: Port Townsend, Washington : Copper Canyon Press, [2019]
Identifiers: LCCN 2018048965 | ISBN 9781556594861 (pbk. : alk. paper)
Classification: LCC PS3602.R699 A6 2019 | DDC 811/.6—dc23
LC record available at https://lccn.loc.gov/2018048965

98765432

COPPER CANYON PRESS
Post Office Box 271
Port Townsend, Washington 98368
www.coppercanyonpress.org

ACKNOWLEDGMENTS

Earlier versions of these poems appeared in the following journals and anthologies: The Academy of American Poets Poem-a-Day, *The American Poetry Review, The Baffler, Bennington Review, The Best American Poetry* 2017, *BOMB Magazine, Boston Review, BuzzFeed, The Georgia Review, The Golden Shovel Anthology: New Poems Honoring Gwendolyn Brooks, Gulf Coast, Memorious, The Nation, The New Criterion, The New Yorker, Opossum, Oxford American, The Paris Review, PEN Poetry Series, Phi Kappa Phi Forum, Poetry, Poetry London,* Poetry Society of America online, *The Rumpus, T: The New York Times Style Magazine, Time, Tin House, TriQuarterly, Vinyl,* and *Weber: The Contemporary West.*

This book was written with the support of the Bread Loaf Writers' Conference, Emory University, the John Simon Guggenheim Foundation, the Poetry Society of America, and the Sewanee Writers' Conference.

In memory of
Bertha Lee Lenoir
(1932–2018)

I will bring you a whole person
and you will bring me a whole person
and we will have us twice as much
of love and everything.

Mari Evans

CONTENTS

I

II

THE TRADITION

Ganymede

A man trades his son for horses.
That's the version I prefer. I like
The safety of it, no one at fault,
Everyone rewarded. God gets
The boy. The boy becomes
Immortal. His father rides until
Grief sounds as good as the gallop
Of an animal born to carry those
Who patrol our inherited
Kingdom. When we look at myth
This way, nobody bothers saying
Rape. I mean, don't you want God
To want you? Don't you dream
Of someone with wings taking you
Up? And when the master comes
For our children, he smells
Like the men who own stables
In Heaven, that far terrain
Between Promise and Apology.
No one has to convince us.
The people of my country believe
We can't be hurt if we can be bought.

As a Human Being

There is the happiness you have
And the happiness you deserve.
They sit apart from each other
The way you and your mother
Sat on opposite ends of the sofa
After an ambulance came to take
Your father away. Some good
Doctor will stitch him up, and
Soon an aunt will arrive to drive
Your mother to the hospital
Where she will settle next to him
Forever, as promised. She holds
The arm of her seat as if she could
Fall, as if it is the only sturdy thing,
And it is, since you've done what
You always wanted, you fought
Your father and won, marred him.
He'll have a scar he can see all
Because of you. And your mother,
The only woman you ever cried for,
Must tend to it as a bride tends
To her vows, forsaking all others
No matter how sore the injury.
No matter how sore the injury
Has left you, you sit understanding
Yourself as a human being finally
Free now that nobody's got to love you.

Flower

Yellow bird.
Yellow house.
Little yellow
Song

Light in my
Jaundiced mouth.
These yellow
Teeth need

Brushing, but
You admire
My yellow
Smile. This

Black boy
Keeps singing.
Tiny life.
Yellow bile.

The Microscopes

Heavy and expensive, hard and black
With bits of chrome, they looked
Like baby cannons, the real children of war, and I
Hated them for that, for what our teacher said
They could do, and then I hated them
For what they did when we gave up
Stealing looks at one another's bodies
To press a left or right eye into the barrel and see
Our actual selves taken down to a cell
Then blown back up again, every atomic thing
About a piece of my coiled hair on one slide
Just as unimportant as anyone else's
Growing in that science
Class where I learned what little difference
God saw if God saw me. It was the start of one fear,
A puny one not much worth mentioning,
Narrow as the pencil tucked behind my ear, lost
When I reached for it
To stab someone I secretly loved: a bigger boy
Who'd advance
Through those tight, locker-lined corridors shoving
Without saying
Excuse me, more an insult than a battle. No large loss.
Not at all. Nothing necessary to study
Or recall. No fighting in the hall
On the way to an American history exam
I almost passed. Redcoats.
Red blood cells. Red-bricked
Education I rode the bus to get. I can't remember
The exact date or

Grade, but I know when I began ignoring slight alarms
That move others to charge or retreat. I'm a kind
Of camouflage. I never let on when scared
Of conflicts so old they seem to amount
To nothing really—dust particles left behind—
Like the viral geography of an occupied territory,
A region I imagine you imagine when you see
A white woman walking with a speck like me.

The Tradition

Aster. Nasturtium. Delphinium. We thought
Fingers in dirt meant it was our dirt, learning
Names in heat, in elements classical
Philosophers said could change us. *Stargazer.*
Foxglove. Summer seemed to bloom against the will
Of the sun, which news reports claimed flamed hotter
On this planet than when our dead fathers
Wiped sweat from their necks. *Cosmos. Baby's Breath.*
Men like me and my brothers filmed what we
Planted for proof we existed before
Too late, sped the video to see blossoms
Brought in seconds, colors you expect in poems
Where the world ends, everything cut down.
John Crawford. Eric Garner. Mike Brown.

Hero

She never knew one of us from another, so my brothers and I grew up
    fighting
Over our mother's mind
Like sun-colored suitors in a Greek myth. We were willing
To do evil. We kept chocolate around our mouths. The last of her
    mother's lot,
She cried at funerals, cried when she whipped me. She whipped me
Daily. I am most interested in people who declare gratitude
For their childhood beatings. None of them took what my mother gave,
Waking us for school with sharp slaps to our bare thighs.
That side of the family is darker. I should be grateful. So I will be—
No one on Earth knows how many abortions happened
Before a woman risked her freedom by giving that risk a name,
By taking it to breast. I don't know why I am alive now
That I still cannot impress the woman who whipped me
Into being. I turned my mother into a grandmother. She thanks me
By kissing my sons. Gratitude is black—
Black as a hero returning from war to a country that banked on his death.
Thank God. It can't get much darker than that.

After *Another Country*

Some dark of us dark,
The ones like me, walk
Around looking for
A building or a bridge.

We mumble and pull
At our lips, convinced,
Until we see how far
Down the distance.

We arrive to leave,
Calling ourselves
Cowards, but not you,
Rufus. You make it

To the George Washington—
Bold as an officer of the law
With the right to direct traffic
When all the stoplights

Are out—and you leap
Dirty against the whiteness
Of the sky to your escape
Through the whiteness

Of the water.

The Water Lilies

They open in the day and close at night.
They are good at appearances. They are white.
I judge them, judge the study they make
Of themselves, aspirational beings, fake
If you ask me. If you ask me, I'll say no,
Thank you, I don't need to watch what goes
Only imagining itself seen, don't need
To see them yawn their thin mouths and feed

On light, absolute and unmoved. They remind
Me of black people who see the movie
About slaves and exit saying how they would
Have fought to whip Legree with his own whip
And walked away from the plantation,
Their eyes raised to the sun, without going blind.

Foreday in the Morning

My mother grew morning glories that spilled onto the walkway
    toward her porch
Because she was a woman with land who showed as much by giving it
    color.
She told me I could have whatever I worked for. That means she was
    an American.
But she'd say it was because she believed
In God. I am ashamed of America
And confounded by God. I thank God for my citizenship in spite
Of the timer set on my life to write
These words: I love my mother. I love black women
Who plant flowers as sheepish as their sons. By the time the blooms
Unfurl themselves for a few hours of light, the women who tend them
Are already at work. Blue. I'll never know who started the lie that we
    are lazy,
But I'd love to wake that bastard up
At foreday in the morning, toss him in a truck, and drive him under
    God
Past every bus stop in America to see all those black folk
Waiting to go work for whatever they want. A house? A boy
To keep the lawn cut? Some color in the yard? My God, we leave
    things green.

The Card Tables

Stop playing. You do remember the card tables,
Slick stick figures like men with low-cut fades,
Short but standing straight
Because we bent them into weak display.
What didn't we want? What wouldn't we claim?
How perfectly each surface was made
For throwing or dropping or slamming a necessary
Portion of our pay.
And how could any of us get by
With one in the way?
Didn't that bare square ask to be played
On, beaten on the head, then folded, then put away,
All so we could call ourselves safe
Now that there was more room, a little more space?

Bullet Points

I will not shoot myself
In the head, and I will not shoot myself
In the back, and I will not hang myself
With a trashbag, and if I do,
I promise you, I will not do it
In a police car while handcuffed
Or in the jail cell of a town
I only know the name of
Because I have to drive through it
To get home. Yes, I may be at risk,
But I promise you, I trust the maggots
Who live beneath the floorboards
Of my house to do what they must
To any carcass more than I trust
An officer of the law of the land
To shut my eyes like a man
Of God might, or to cover me with a sheet
So clean my mother could have used it
To tuck me in. When I kill me, I will
Do it the same way most Americans do,
I promise you: cigarette smoke
Or a piece of meat on which I choke
Or so broke I freeze
In one of these winters we keep
Calling worst. I promise if you hear
Of me dead anywhere near
A cop, then that cop killed me. He took
Me from us and left my body, which is,
No matter what we've been taught,
Greater than the settlement

A city can pay a mother to stop crying,
And more beautiful than the new bullet
Fished from the folds of my brain.

Duplex

A poem is a gesture toward home.
It makes dark demands I call my own.

      Memory makes demands darker than my own:
      My last love drove a burgundy car.

My first love drove a burgundy car.
He was fast and awful, tall as my father.

      Steadfast and awful, my tall father
      Hit hard as a hailstorm. He'd leave marks.

Light rain hits easy but leaves its own mark
Like the sound of a mother weeping again.

      Like the sound of my mother weeping again,
      No sound beating ends where it began.

None of the beaten end up how we began.
A poem is a gesture toward home.

The Trees

In my front yard live three crape myrtles, *crying trees*
We once called them, not the shadiest but soothing
During a break from work in the heat, their cool sweat

Falling into us. I don't want to make more of it.
I'd like to let these spindly things be
Since my gift for transformation here proves

Useless now that I know everyone moves the same
Whether moving in tears or moving
To punch my face. A crape myrtle is

A crape myrtle. Three is a family. It is winter. They are bare.
It's not that I love them
Every day. It's that I love them anyway.

Second Language

You come with a little
Black string tied
Around your tongue,
Knotted to remind
Where you came from
And why you left
Behind photographs
Of people whose
Names now buck
Pronouncing. How
Do you say God
Now that the night
Rises sooner? Why
Must we wake to work
Before any alarm?
I am the man asking,
The great-grandson
Made so by the dead
Tenant farmers promised
A plot of woods to hew.
They thought they could
Own the dirt they were
Bound to. In that part
Of the country, a knot
Is something you get
After getting knocked
Down, and story means
Lie. In your plot
Of the country, class
Means school, this room

Where we practice
Words that undo your
Tongue when you tell
A lie or start a promise
Or unravel like a story.

After Avery R. Young

Blk is not a country, but I live there
Where even the youngest call you baby.
Sometimes you ain't we. Sometimes you is
Everybody. Washboard rains come. We
Open our mouths for a drink. Rather be radical
Than a fool. Oh and no,
We're not interested in killing
White people or making them
Work. Matter of truth, some snorted
Cocaine until folk started calling it
White lady. Slavery is a bad idea.
The more you look like me, the more we
Agree. Sometimes you is everybody.
The blk mind is a continuous
Mind. There is a we. I am among them.
I am one of the ones. I belong. Oom boom
Ba boom. I live there where
We have a right to expect something of the brother.
Hooking and crooking or punching the clock,
It's got to get done. That
Expectation. Stunning. Incantatory. Blk.
Power in our 24-hour
Barbershops. Power in the Stateville
Correctional Center. Power broke
Whether I have a car note or not.
Power under a quilt that won't unravel, though
I never met the woman who sewed it
Or the woman for whom it was a gift
Before it finally came to me. The blk mind
Is a continuous mind. I am not a narrative

Form, but dammit if I don't tell a story.
All land owned is land once stolen.
So the blues people of the world walk
On water. We will not die. Blk music.
Blk rage. Blk city of the soul
In a very cold town. Blk ice is ice you can't see.

A Young Man

We stand together on our block, me and my son,
Neighbors saying our face is the same, but I know
He's better than me: when other children move

Toward my daughter, he lurches like a brother
Meant to put them down. He is a bodyguard
On the playground. He won't turn apart from her,

Empties any enemy, leaves them flimsy, me
Confounded. I never fought for so much—
I calmed my daughter when I could cradle

My daughter; my son swaggers about her.
He won't have to heal a girl he won't let free.
They are so small. And I, still, am a young man.

In him lives my black anger made red.
They play. He is not yet incarcerated.

Duplex

The opposite of rape is understanding
A field of flowers called paintbrushes—

A field of flowers called paintbrushes,
Though the spring be less than actual.

Though the spring be less than actual,
Men roam shirtless as if none ever hurt me.

Men roam that myth. In truth, one hurt me.
I want to obliterate the flowered field,

To obliterate my need for the field
And raise a building above the grasses,

A building of prayer against the grasses,
My body a temple in disrepair.

My body is a temple in disrepair.
The opposite of rape is understanding.

Riddle

We do not recognize the body
Of Emmett Till. We do not know
The boy's name nor the sound
Of his mother wailing. We have
Never heard a mother wailing.
We do not know the history
Of this nation in ourselves. We
Do not know the history of our-
Selves on this planet because
We do not have to know what
We believe we own. We believe
We own your bodies but have no
Use for your tears. We destroy
The body that refuses use. We use
Maps we did not draw. We see
A sea so cross it. We see a moon
So land there. We love land so
Long as we can take it. Shhh. We
Can't take that sound. What is
A mother wailing? We do not
Recognize music until we can
Sell it. We sell what cannot be
Bought. We buy silence. Let us
Help you. How much does it cost
To hold your breath underwater?
Wait. Wait. What are we? What?
What on Earth are we? What?

Good White People

Not my phrase, I swear,
But my grandmother's
When someone surprised her
By holding open the door
Or by singing that same high C
Stephanie Mills holds
Near the end of "I Have Learned
To Respect the Power of Love"
Or by gifting her with a turkey
On the 24th of December
After a year of not tipping her
For cleaning what they could afford
Not to clean. You'll have to forgive
My grandmother with her *good*
Hair and her *good white people*
And her certified *good slap across*
Your mouth. Crack the beaten door
To eat or sing, but do not speak
Evil. Dead bad black woman
I still love, she didn't know
What we know. In America
Today, anyone can turn on
A TV or look out a window
To see several kinds of bird
In the air while each face watching
Smiles and spits, cusses and sings
A single anthem of blood—
All is stained. She was ugly.
I'm ugly. You're ugly too.
No such thing as good white people.

Correspondence

after *The Jerome Project* by Titus Kaphar
(oil, gold leaf, and tar on wood panels;
7" × 10½" each)

I am writing to you from the other side
Of my body where I have never been
Shot and no one's ever cut me.
I had to go back this far in order
To present myself as a whole being
You'd heed and believe in. You can trust me
When I am young. You can know more
When you move your hands over a child,
Swift and without the interruptions
We associate with penetration.
The young are hard for you
To kill. May be harder still to hear a kid cry
Without looking for a sweet
To slip into his mouth. Won't you hold him?
Won't you coo toward the years before my story
Is all the fault of our imaginations?
We can make me
Better if you like: write back. Or take the trip.
I've dressed my wounds with tar
And straightened a place for you
On the cold side of this twin bed.

Trojan

When a hurricane sends
Winds far enough north
To put our power out,
We only think of winning
The war bodies wage
To prove the border
Between them isn't real.
An act of God, so sweet.
No TV. No novel. No
Recreation but each
Other, and neither of us
Willing to kill. I don't care
That I don't love my lover.
Knowing where to stroke
In little light, knowing what
Will happen to me and how
Soon, these rank higher
Than a clear view
Of the face I'd otherwise
Flay had I some training
In combat, a blade, a few
Matches. Candles are
Romantic because
We understand shadows.
We recognize the shape
Of what once made us
Come, so we come
Thinking of approach
In ways that forgo
Substance. I'm breathing—

Heaving now—
In my own skin, and I
Know it. Romance is
An act. The perimeter
Stays intact. We make out
So little that I can't help
But imagine my safety.
I get to tell the truth
About what kind
Of a person lives and who
Dies. Barefoot survivors.
Damned heroes, each
Corpse lit on a pyre.
Patroclus died because
He could not see
What he really was inside
His lover's armor.

The Legend of *Big* and *Fine*

Long ago, we used two words
For the worth of a house, a car,
A woman—all the same to men
Who claimed them: things
To be entered, each to suffer
Wear and tear with time, but
Greater than the love for these
Was the strong little grin
One man offered another
Saying, *You lucky. You got you*
A big, fine _____.
Hard to imagine so many men
Waiting on each other to be
Recognized, every crooked
Tooth in our naming mouths
Ready like the syllables
Of a very short sentence, all
Of us crying *mine,* like babies who
Grab for what must be beautiful
Since someone else saw it.

The Peaches

I choose these two, bruised—
Maybe too ripe to take, fondling
As I toss them each
Into my cart, the smaller
With its stem somewhat
Intact—because they remind me
Of the girls who won't be girls
Much longer, both sealed
And secured like a monarch's
Treasure in a basement below
The basement of the house
I inherited. I've worked hard and want
To bring them something sweet
So they know I've missed them
More than anyone else. But first,
I weigh the peaches, pay
For them, make the short drive
To my childhood
Home of latches, mazes,
And locked doors. Every key
Mine now, though I've hidden a few
From myself. I pride myself
On my gifts. I can fashion for you
A place to play, and when you think
It's dark there, I hand you
Fruit like two swollen bulbs
Of light you can hold on to,
Watch your eyes brighten as you eat.

Night Shift

When I am touched, brushed, and measured, I think of myself
As a painting. The artist works no matter the lack of sleep. I am made
Beautiful. I never eat. I once bothered with a man who called me
Snack, Midnight Snack to be exact. I'd oblige because he hurt me
With a violence I mistook for desire. I'd get left hanging
In one room of his dim house while he swept or folded laundry.
When you've been worked on for so long, you never know
You're done. Paint dries. Midnight is many colors. Black and blue
Are only two. The man who tinted me best kept me looking a little
Like a chore. How do you say *prepared*
In French? How do you draw a man on the night shift? Security
At the museum for the blind, he eats to stay
Awake. He's so full, he never has to eat again. And the moon goes.

Shovel

I am not the man who put a bullet in its brain,
But I am commissioned to dispose of the corpse:
Lay furniture plastic next to it and roll it over
Until it is wrapped, tape with duct tape until
It is completely contained, lay next to that
Containment a tarp and roll it over until it is
Wrapped again, take cheap hardware twine
And tie it and tie it like a proper gift, a gift
A good child will give up on opening
Even come Christmas morning. I am here
To ignore the stench and throw the dead over
My left shoulder and carry it to the bed
Of a stolen truck. I did not steal the truck,
But there it is, outside the door, engine
Running. I do the driving and assume someone
Else must scrub the floors of the body's blood,
Scrub the body's last room of its evidence.
I do the driving and sing whatever love songs
The truck's radio affords me all the way
To the edge of anywhere hiking families refuse
To wander, and I dig and dig and dig as
Undertakers did before the advent of machinery,
Then lift, again, the dead, and throw, again,
The dead—quite tired now, winded really,
But my hands and shoulders and arms and legs
Unstoppable. I dump the body into the hole
I myself made, and I hum, some days, one
Of those love songs, some days, a song I myself
Make in my spinning head, which is wet
With sweat that drips into the hole I will not call

A grave. I sweat into the earth as I repair it.
I completely cover the dead before I return
The truck where I assume someone else must
Scrub it—engine off—of the body's evidence,
And I sing, again, those songs because I know
The value of sweet music when we need to pass
The time without wondering what rots beneath our feet.

The Long Way

Your grandfather was a murderer.
I'm glad he's dead.

He invented the toothbrush,
But I don't care to read his name

On the building I walk through

To avoid the rain. He raped women
Who weren't yet women.

I imagine the wealth he left
When you turn red. I imagine you as a baby

Bouncing on a rapist's knee. I like my teeth
Clean. I like to stay warm

And healthy. I get it. Then I get it
Again: my oral hygiene and your memory

Avoiding each other

Like a girl who walks the long way
To miss the neighborhood bully, like the bully

Who'd really rather beat up on somebody
New. I can't help you. I can't hug you.

I can't grip your right hand, though
It never held a gun, though it never

Covered a lovely mouth, and you can't pay me
To cross the ground floor without wishing

I could spit on or mar some slick surface

And not think of who will have to do the cleaning.
We'd all still be poor. I'd end up drenched

Going around. You'd end remembering
What won't lead to a smile that gleams

In dark places. Some don't know
How dark. Some do.

Dear Whiteness

Come, love, come lie down, love, with me
In this king-size bed where we go numb
For each other letting sleep take us into
Ease, a slumber made only when I hold
You or you hold me so close I have no idea
Where I begin—where do you end?—where you

Tell me lies. Tell me sweet little lies

About what I mean to you when
I've labored all day and wish to come
Home like a war hero who lost an arm.
That's how I fight to win you, to gain
Ground you are welcome to divide
And name. See how this mouth opens
To speak what language you allow me
With the threat of my head cradled safe.

Tell me lies. Tell me sweet little lies

Of what you require, intimacy so industrious
That when I wake to brush you from my own
Teeth I see you in the mirror. I won't stay
Too long. When you look in that mirror, it
Will be clean. You'll be content
Seeing only yourself. Was I ever there?

Tell me lies. Tell me. Tell me lies.

Of the Swan

The luck of it: my ordinary body
Once under

A god. No night ends his
Care, how

He finishes a fixed field, how he
Hollows

A low tunnel. He released me
After. Why

Else pray like a woman
Ruined

By an ever-bitter extremity?
Men die,

But God's soul rises out of its black
Noose, finds

Bared skin a landscape prepared
For use—

Immortality requires worship.
I was

The Lord's opening on Earth,
A woman

With feathers strewn round
My hide.

Entertainment Industry

Scared to see a movie
All the way through
       I got to scream each scene
       Duck and get down
       Mass shooting blues

When you see me coming
You see me running
When you see me running
You run too

I don't have kids
Cuz I'd have to send them to school
       Ain't that safe as any
       Plan for parenthood
       Mass shooting blues

When you see me coming
You see me running
If you can beat a bullet
You oughta run too

Stake

I am a they in most of America.
Someone feels lost in the forest
Of we, so he can't imagine
A single tree. He can't bear it.
A cross. A crucifixion. Such
A Christian. All that wood
Headed his way in the fact
Of a man or a woman who
Might as well be a secret, so
Serious his need to see inside.
To cut down. To tell. How
Old will I get to be in a nation
That believes we can grow out
Of a grave? Can reach. Climb
High as the First State Bank.
Take a bullet. Break through
Concrete. The sidewalk.
The street someone crosses
When he sees wilderness where
He wanted his city. His cross-
Tie. His telephone pole.
Timber. Timbre. It's an awful
Sound, and people pay to hear
It. People say bad things about
Me, though they don't know
My name. I have a name.
A stake. I settle. Dig. Die.
Go underground. Tunnel
The ocean floor. Root. Shoot
Up like a thought someone
Planted. Someone planted

An idea of me. A lie. A lawn
Jockey. The myth of a wooded
Hamlet in America, a thicket,
Hell, a patch of sunlit grass
Where any one of us bursts into
One someone as whole as we.

Layover

Dallas is so
Far away
Even for the people
Who live
In Dallas a hub
Through which we get
To smaller places
That lurch
And hurt going
Home means stopping
In Dallas and all are
From little
Towns and farms
If all keep
Heading back
Far enough pay
Attention keep
Your belongings
Near everyone
In Dallas is
Still driving
At 3:24 a.m.
Off I-20 where
I was raped
Though no one
Would call it
That he was
Hovering by
The time
I understood

He thought it necessary
To leave me with knowledge
I can be
Hated I was
Smaller then
One road went
Through me
No airport
I drove
Him home
A wreck
On the freeway
We sat
In traffic
My wallet
On the seat
In between
My legs

Duplex

I begin with love, hoping to end there.
I don't want to leave a messy corpse.

      I don't want to leave a messy corpse
      Full of medicines that turn in the sun.

Some of my medicines turn in the sun.
Some of us don't need hell to be good.

      Those who need most, need hell to be good.
      What are the symptoms of *your* sickness?

Here is one symptom of my sickness:
Men who love me are men who miss me.

      Men who leave me are men who miss me
      In the dream where I am an island.

In the dream where I am an island,
I grow green with hope. I'd like to end there.

Of My Fury

I love a man I know could die
And not by way of illness
And not by his own hand
But because of the color of that hand and all
His flawless skin. One joy in it is
Understanding he can hurt me
But won't. I thought by now I'd be unhappy
Unconscious next to the same lover
So many nights in a row. He readies
For bed right on the other side
Of my fury, but first, I make a braid of us.
I don't sleep until I get what I want.

After Essex Hemphill

The night is the night. So
Say the stars that light us
As we kneel illegal and
Illegal like Malcolm X.
This is his park, this part
Of the capital where we
Say please with our mouths
Full of each other, no one
Hungry as me against this
Tree. This tree, if we push
Too hard, will fall. But if
I don't push at all, call me
A sissy. Somebody ahead
Of me seeded the fruit-
Bearing forest. The night
Is my right. Shouldn't I
Eat? Shouldn't I repeat,
It was good, like God?

Stay

> It was restful, learning nothing necessary.
> *Gwendolyn Brooks*

All day, I kept still just to think of it—

Your body above mine, what was
A lack of air between us—hot but restful

As I sat center on my bed of learning,

Mouth open, touching nothing,
My memory the only noise necessary.

A.D.

Each wounds you badly, but no boy hurts
Like the first one

                    When you slept in a bed
Too narrow for two. You thought he disappeared

                In the sheet and cushion,
But look at you now, twenty-eight in a king, you wake

With a man on your mind— Head
On your chest, both of you bent

As best you can to make
Room for the other.

Ten years, your feet hanging, tangled and long, and still
You're the victim

Of such nightmares. You breathe
Like he's been lying

                    On top for the last decade.
A man goes to heaven, you suffocate below the weight.

Turn You Over

All my anxiety is separation anxiety.
I want to believe you are here with me,
But the bed is bigger and the trash
Overflows. Someone righteous should
Take out my garbage. I am so many odd
And enviable things. Righteous is not
One of them. I'd rather a man to avoid
Than a man to imagine in a realm
Unseen, though even the doctor who
Shut your eyes swears you're somewhere
As close as breath. Mine, not yours.
You don't have breath. You got
Heaven. That's supposed to be my
Haven. I want you to tell me it sparkles
There. I want you to tell me anything
Again and again while I turn you over
To quiet you or to wake and remind you
I can't be expected to clean up after a man.

The Virus

Dubbed undetectable, I can't kill
The people you touch, and I can't
Blur your view
Of the pansies you've planted
Outside the window, meaning
I can't kill the pansies, but I want to.
I want them dying, and I want
To do the killing. I want you
To heed that I'm still here
Just beneath your skin and in
Each organ
The way anger dwells in a man
Who studies the history of his nation.
If I can't leave you
Dead, I'll have
You vexed. Look. Look
Again: show me the color
Of your flowers now.

The Rabbits

I caught them
In couples on the lawn
As I pulled into my driveway
After a night of bare music,
Of drinking on my feet
Because I think I look better
Standing. I should lie. Say
They expressed my desire
To mount and be
Mounted as they scurried
Into the darkest parts of what
I pay for, but I am tired
Of claiming beauty where
There is only truth: the rabbits
Heard me coming and said
Danger in whatever tongue
Stops them from making
More. I should say
I understood myself
That way, as danger, engine
Idling, but I thought
Infestation. Now I worry
No one will ever love me—
Furry little delights fucking
In my own front yard and I,
I am reminded of all I've gotten
Rid of. And every living
Thing that still must go.

Monotheism

Some people need religion. Me?
I've got my long black hair. I twist
The roots and braid it tight. *You're*

My villain. You're a hard father, from
Behind, it whines, tied and tucked,
Untouchable. Then comes

The night— Before I carry my
Mane to bed with me, I sit us
In front of the vanity. Undo. Un-

Wind. *Finally your fingers,* it says
Near my ear, *Your fingers. Your*
Whole hands. No one's but yours.

Token

Burg, boro, ville, and wood,
I hate those tiny towns,
Their obligations. If I needed
Anyone to look at me, I'd dye my hair purple
And live in Bemidji. Look at me. I want to dye
My hair purple and never notice
You notice. I want the scandal
In my bedroom but not in the mouths of convenience
Store customers off the nearest highway. Let me be
Another invisible,
Used and forgotten and left
To whatever narrow miseries I make for myself
Without anybody asking
What's wrong. Concern for my soul offends me, so
I live in the city, the very shape of it
Winding like the mazes of the adult-video outlets
I roamed in my twenties: pay a token to walk through
Tunnels of men, quick and colorless there where we
Each knew what we were,
There where I wasn't the only one.

The Hammers

They sat on the dresser like anything
I put in my pocket before leaving
The house. I even saw a few little ones
Tilted against the window of my living
Room, metal threats with splinters
For handles. They leaned like those
Teenage boys at the corner who might
Not be teenage boys because they ask
For dollars in the middle of the early
April day and because they knock
At 10 a.m. Do I need help lifting some-
Thing heavy? Yard work? The boys
Seemed not to care that they lay
On the floor lit by the TV. I'd have
Covered them up with linen, with dry
Towels and old coats, but their claw
And sledge and ball-peen heads shone
In the dark, which is, at least, a view
In the dark. And their handles meant
My hands, striking surfaces, getting
Shelves up, finally. One hung
From the narrow end of a spoke
In the ceiling fan, in wait of summer.
I found another propped near the bulb
In the refrigerator. Wasn't I hungry?
Why have them there if I could not
Use them, if I could not look at my own
Reflection in the mirror and take one
To the temple and knock myself out?

I Know What I Love

It comes from the earth.
It is green with deceit.
Sometimes what I love
Shows up at three
In the morning and
Rushes in to turn me
Upside down. Some-
Times what I love just
Doesn't show up at all.
It can hurt me if it
Means to… because
That's what *in love*
Means. What I love
Understands itself
As properly scarce.
It knows I can't need
What I don't go without.
Some nights I hold
My breath. I turn as in
Go bad. When I die
A man or a woman will
Clean up the mess
A body makes. They'll
Talk about gas prices
And the current drought
As they prepare the blue-
Black cadaver that still,
As the dead do, groans:
I wanted what anyone
With an ear wants—
To be touched and

Touched by a presence
That has no hands.

Crossing

The water is one thing, and one thing for miles.
The water is one thing, making this bridge
Built over the water another. Walk it
Early, walk it back when the day goes dim, everyone
Rising just to find a way toward rest again.
We work, start on one side of the day
Like a planet's only sun, our eyes straight
Until the flame sinks. The flame sinks. Thank God
I'm different. I've figured and counted. I'm not crossing
To cross back. I'm set
On something vast. It reaches
Long as the sea. I'm more than a conqueror, bigger
Than bravery. I don't march. I'm the one who leaps.

Deliverance

Though I have not shined shoes for it,
Have not suffocated myself handsome
In a tight, bright tie, Sunday comes
To me again as it did in childhood.

We few left who listen to the radio leave
Ourselves available to surprise. We pray
Unaware of prayer. We are an ugly people.

Forgive me, I do not wish to sing
Like Tramaine Hawkins, but Lord if I could
Become the note she belts halfway into
The fifth minute of "The Potter's House"

When black vocabulary heralds home-
Made belief: *For any kind of havoc, there is*
Deliverance! She means that even after I am

Not listening. I am not a saint
Because I keep trying to be a sound, something
You will remember
Once you've lived enough not to believe in heaven.

Meditations at the New Orleans Jazz
National Historical Park

1

Dear Tom Dent,
We still love you
And love what
It means to be
A black college
President's son
Whose pride
And rebellion
Look like men
In the Seventh Ward.
They groaned
For you, and
Ain't that music
Too, bodies
Of several
Shades arranged
For one sound
Of want or
Without or *wish*
A Negro would— Come
Back home,
Little light
Skin, come
Give Daddy
A kiss.

2

I present myself that you might

Understand how you got here
And who you owe. As long as

I can remember the brass band, it
Lives, every goodbye a lie. Every
One of them carries the weight

He chose. And plays it. No theft.
No rape. No flood. No. Not in
This moment. Not in this lovely

Sunlit room of my mind. Holy.

So the Bible says, in the beginning,
Blackness. I am alive. You?
Alive. You born with the nerve

To arrive yawning. You who
Walk without noticing your feet
On an early morning swept hard-

Wood floor: because Eve, because
Lucy. The whole toe of my boot,

Tapping.

3
This chair
Is where
I understand
I am
Nothing if
I can't
Sit awhile
In the audience
Or alone, sit
Down awhile
And thank God
The seat
Has stayed
Warm.

Dark

I am sick of your sadness,
Jericho Brown, your blackness,
Your books. Sick of you
Laying me down
So I forget how sick
I am. I'm sick of your good looks,
Your debates, your concern, your
Determination to keep your butt
Plump, the little money you earn.
I'm sick of you saying no when yes is as easy
As a young man, bored with you
Saying yes to every request
Though you're as tired as anyone else yet
Consumed with a single
Diagnosis of health. I'm sick
Of your hurting. I see that
You're blue. You may be ugly,
But that ain't new.
Everyone you know is
Just as cracked. Everyone you love is
As dark, or at least as black.

Duplex

Don't accuse me of sleeping with your man
When I didn't know you had a man.

       Back when I didn't know you had a man,
       The moon glowed above the city's blackout.

I walked home by moonlight through the blackout.
I was too young to be reasonable.

       He was so young, so unreasonable,
       He dipped weed in embalming fluid.

He'd dip our weed in embalming fluid.
We'd make love on trains and in dressing rooms.

       Love in the subway, love in mall restrooms.
       A bore at home, he transformed in the city.

What's yours at home is a wolf in my city.
You can't accuse me of sleeping with a man.

Thighs and Ass

Where I am my thickest, I grew
Myself by squat and lunge, and all

The time I sweated, I did not think
Of being divided or entered, though

Yes, I knew meat would lure men,
And flesh properly placed will lead

One to think that he can—when
He runs from what sniffs to kill us—

Mount my back trusting I may carry
Him at a good speed for a long distance,

And to believe, believe that
When he hungers, I am able

To leap high, snatch
The fruit of the tree

We pause to hide behind and feed, feed him.

Cakewalk

My man swears his HIV is better than mine, that his has in it a little
gold, something he can spend if he ever gets old, claims mine is full
of lead: slows you down, he tells me, looking over his shoulder. But
I keep my eyes on his behind, say my HIV is just fine. Practical. Like
pennies. Like copper. It can conduct electricity. Keep the heat on or
shock you. It works hard, earns as much as my smile.

Stand

Peace on this planet
Or guns glowing hot,
We lay there together
As if we were getting
Something done. It
Felt like planting
A garden or planning
A meal for a people
Who still need feeding,
All that touching or
Barely touching, not
Saying much, not adding
Anything. The cushion
Of it, the skin and
Occasional sigh, all
Seemed like work worth
Mastering. I'm sure
Somebody died while
We made love. Some-
Body killed somebody
Black. I thought then
Of holding you
As a political act. I
May as well have
Held myself. We didn't
Stand for one thought,
Didn't do a damn thing,
And though you left
Me, I'm glad we didn't.

Duplex: Cento

My last love drove a burgundy car,
Color of a rash, a symptom of sickness.

> We were the symptoms, the road our sickness:
> None of our fights ended where they began.

None of the beaten end where they begin.
Any man in love can cause a messy corpse,

> But I didn't want to leave a messy corpse
> Obliterated in some lilied field,

Stench obliterating lilies of the field,
The murderer, young and unreasonable.

> He was so young, so unreasonable,
> Steadfast and awful, tall as my father.

Steadfast and awful, my tall father
Was my first love. He drove a burgundy car.

NOTES

The italicized portion of "After Avery R. Young" is a 2010 quotation from Louis Farrakhan, the leader of the Nation of Islam (which has its headquarters in Chicago, Illinois).

The italicized lines in "Dear Whiteness" are from "Little Lies" by Fleetwood Mac from the album *Tango in the Night* (Warner Bros. Records, 1987).

"Duplex (I begin with…)" is for L. Lamar Wilson.

"The Hammers" is modeled after "What the Angels Left" by Marie Howe.

ABOUT THE AUTHOR

Jericho Brown is the recipient of a Whiting Award and of fellowships from the John Simon Guggenheim Foundation, the Radcliffe Institute for Advanced Study at Harvard University, and the National Endowment for the Arts. His poems have appeared in *Fence, jubilat, The New Criterion, The New Republic, The New Yorker, The New York Times, Time,* and several of *The Best American Poetry* anthologies. His first book, *Please* (New Issues, 2008), won the American Book Award. His second book, *The New Testament* (Copper Canyon, 2014), won the Anisfield-Wolf Book Award. He serves as poetry editor for *The Believer.* He is an associate professor of English and Creative Writing and Director of the Creative Writing Program at Emory University in Atlanta.

Lannan Literary Selections

For two decades Lannan Foundation has supported the publication and distribution of exceptional literary works. Copper Canyon Press gratefully acknowledges their support.

LANNAN LITERARY SELECTIONS 2019

Jericho Brown, *The Tradition*

Deborah Landau, *Soft Targets*

Paisley Rekdal, *Nightingale*

Natalie Scenters-Zapico, *Lima :: Limón*

Matthew Zapruder, *Father's Day*

RECENT LANNAN LITERARY SELECTIONS FROM COPPER CANYON PRESS

Sherwin Bitsui, *Dissolve*

Marianne Boruch, *Cadaver, Speak*

John Freeman, *Maps*

Jenny George, *The Dream of Reason*

Ha Jin, *A Distant Center*

Deborah Landau, *The Uses of the Body*

Maurice Manning, *One Man's Dark*

Rachel McKibbens, *blud*

W.S. Merwin, *The Lice*

Aimee Nezhukumatathil, *Oceanic*

Camille Rankine, *Incorrect Merciful Impulses*

Paisley Rekdal, *Imaginary Vessels*

Brenda Shaughnessy, *So Much Synth*

Frank Stanford, *What About This: Collected Poems of Frank Stanford*

Ocean Vuong, *Night Sky with Exit Wounds*

C.D. Wright, *Casting Deep Shade*

Javier Zamora, *Unaccompanied*

Ghassan Zaqtan (translated by Fady Joudah), *The Silence That Remains*

Poetry is vital to language and living. Since 1972, Copper Canyon Press has published extraordinary poetry from around the world to engage the imaginations and intellects of readers, writers, booksellers, librarians, teachers, students, and donors.

WE ARE GRATEFUL FOR THE MAJOR SUPPORT PROVIDED BY:

THE PAUL G. ALLEN
FAMILY FOUNDATION

Anonymous (3)

Jill Baker and Jeffrey Bishop

Anne and Geoffrey Barker

Donna and Matt Bellew

John Branch

Diana Broze

The Beatrice R. and Joseph A. Coleman Foundation, Inc.

Laurie and Oskar Eustis

Mimi Gardner Gates

Nancy Gifford

Gull Industries, Inc. on behalf of William True

The Trust of Warren A. Gummow

Petunia Charitable Fund and advisor Elizabeth Hebert

Bruce Kahn

Phil Kovacevich and Eric Wechsler

Lakeside Industries, Inc.
on behalf of Jeanne Marie Lee

Maureen Lee and Mark Busto

TO LEARN MORE ABOUT UNDERWRITING
COPPER CANYON PRESS TITLES,
PLEASE CALL 360-385-4925 EXT. 103

WE ARE GRATEFUL FOR THE MAJOR SUPPORT PROVIDED BY:

Rhoady Lee and Alan Gartenhaus

Peter Lewis

Ellie Mathews and Carl Youngmann as The North Press

Hank Meijer

Gregg Orr

Gay Phinny

Suzie Rapp and Mark Hamilton

Emily and Dan Raymond

Jill and Bill Ruckelshaus

Kim and Jeff Seely

Richard Swank

Dan Waggoner

Barbara and Charles Wright

Caleb Young as C. Young Creative

The dedicated interns and faithful volunteers
of Copper Canyon Press

The Chinese character for poetry is made up of two parts:
"word" and "temple." It also serves as pressmark for
Copper Canyon Press.

The poems are set Fournier.
Book design and composition by Phil Kovacevich.

CPSIA information can be obtained
at www.ICGtesting.com
Printed in the USA
BVHW030812181220
595868BV00045B/37